WALKS FOR ALL AGES
HAMPSHIRE

WALKS FOR ALL AGES

HAMPSHIRE

Hugh Taylor & Moira McCrossan

BRADWELL
BOOKS

Published by Bradwell Books
9 Orgreave Close Sheffield S13 9NP
Email: books@bradwellbooks.co.uk

1st Edition
Reprinted August 2017

ISBN: 9781910551424

Print: Gomer Press, Llandysul, Ceredigion SA44 4JL

Design by: Andrew Caffrey. **Typesetting by:** Mark Titterton

Photograph Credits: Photographs © Hugh Taylor and Moira McCrossan.
Front Cover courtesy Jane Austin's House Museum
Other images are credited separately.

Maps: Contain Ordnance Survey data
© Crown copyright and database right 2016

Ordnance Survey licence number 100039353

The information in this book has been produced in good faith and is intended as a general guide. Although the maps in this book are based on original Ordnance Survey mapping, walkers are always advised to use a detailed OS map. Look in 'The Basics' section for recommendations for the most suitable map for each of the walks.

Bradwell Books and the authors have made all reasonable efforts to ensure that the details are correct at the time of publication. Bradwell Books and the authors cannot accept responsibility for any changes that have taken place subsequent to the book being published.

It is the responsibility of individuals undertaking any of the walks listed in this book to exercise due care and consideration for their own health and wellbeing and that of others in their party. The walks in this book are not especially strenuous, but individuals taking part should ensure they are fit and well before setting off.

A good pair of walking books is essential for these walks. It is advisable to take good-quality waterproofs, and if undertaking the walks during the winter, take plenty of warm clothing as well. Because the walks will take some time, it would be a good idea to take along some food and drink.

Enjoy walking. Enjoy Hampshire with Bradwell Books!

CONTENTS

INTRODUCTION

Hampshire has pretty villages, clear rivers, ancient cities and the New Forest. You can walk through thousands of years of English history, surveying the marks that generations have made on the land. Iron Age forts were re-used as Roman settlements, which decayed when the Romans left but became prosperous again under Alfred the Great, only to fall to the conquering Normans. Winchester has traces of all this history from Iron Age forts to Norman cathedrals. You can still see the ground plan of the Saxon Old Minster alongside the massive Norman cathedral.

In the cathedral you will find the grave of Jane Austen, one of the most admired English writers of all time. She loved Hampshire and spent most of her life here. You can visit her home in the village of Chawton. This countryside has inspired many writers over the years. Richard Adams based **Watership Down** on Hampshire's rolling farmland and you can walk past Nuthanger Farm, which features in the book. Although Flora Thompson's **Lark Rise to Candleford** was based on her Oxfordshire childhood, she loved the downs around Liphook, which she described in **The Peverel Papers**. Ruth Rendell's and Agatha Christie's fictional detectives were based in Hampshire and you can visit the places which became St Mary Mead and Kingsmarkham in the books and films. Nether Wallop does not seem a likely location for so much death and destruction but equally lovely parts of Hampshire have real histories of murder most foul.

By the Avon River, Alice Lisle gave shelter to two runaways from the Battle of Sedgemoor and was sentenced to death for treason. She was executed at Winchester, where a plaque marks the spot. Eight-year-old Fanny Adams was brutally murdered at Alton, where Parliamentarian soldiers had once attacked the church. In the peaceful New Forest you can walk past World War II bomb craters and you can consider whether William Rufus's death in 1100 was accident or assassination.

The New Forest was created by William, the Conqueror, William Rufus's father, as a royal hunting ground. However, commoners were granted certain rights including the right to pasture their animals. The pastureland and heathland in the National Park are the result of continued grazing by the horses and cattle of the commoners over the centuries. The park has the largest remaining area of common land in England, where the famed New Forest ponies graze everywhere, including by roadsides and over garden fences.

iStock

ECCHINSWELL

Explore the countryside that inspired Richard Adams to write *Watership Down*.

Watership Down, Richard Adams's 1972 novel, is a story about rabbits. One of the rabbits, Fiver, has second sight and foresees the destruction of their warren. Naturally none of the senior rabbits listen to his plea so he and his brother, Hazel, gather a small group of rabbits and set out to find a new home on their own.

Hazel leads the new group, which contains Silver and Bigwig, two former members of the warren's military caste, on the adventure to pastures new. They confront many dangers on the way but hold fast to Fiver's vision of a new safe home for them. Eventually they arrive at Watership Down, where they establish a new warren. Then some other rabbits from the old warren arrive and inform them that Fiver was right and humans destroyed their entire warren.

But all is not well in the new warren. There are no female rabbits and to ensure that the community can continue a search is started to find some females. Among other options Hazel and a rabbit called Pipkin find two pairs of domesticated rabbits in hutches at nearby Nuthanger Farm, which you will pass on this walk. A raid is organised and two females and a male are helped to escape the farm and subsequently join the warren. There is much more to this fascinating story, which started with Richard Adams telling tales of rabbits to his daughters. Adams grew up in Hampshire and his stories of rabbits, 'improvised off the top of my head', were based in part on his own experiences in World War II, in Arnhem, during the Battle of Oosterbeek but set in a location he was very familiar with.

His girls implored him to write the stories down and tormented him until he did so. He sent the manuscript to six publishers, who all rejected it, until the one-man-band publisher Rex Collings decided to take a chance on it. It became a bestseller and has been translated into eighteen languages. In 1978 it was made into a hugely successful animated film. Richard Briers voiced Fiver, John Hurt was Hazel and other characters used the voices of Ralph Richardson, Roy Kinnear, Zero Mostel and Hannah Gordon. The theme song, Mike Batt's 'Bright Eyes', sung by Art Garfunkel, was the biggest selling UK single of 1979.

THE BASICS

Distance: 2½ miles / 4km

Gradient: One easy ascent and descent

Severity: Easy, but some paths can be a bit overgrown in summer

Approx. time to walk: 1¼ hours

Stiles: Two

Map: OS Explorer 144 (Basingstoke)

Path description: Country lanes and woodland and field paths

Start point: Car park in Ecchinswell (GR SU 499596)

Parking: Opposite the school (RG20 4UB)

Dog friendly: Yes (stiles can be avoided if necessary)

Toilets: None on walk

Nearest food: The Royal Oak at Ecchinswell

ECCHINSWELL WALK

1. From the parking go along Mill Lane alongside the school. This becomes a grassy lane and then a footpath. Follow the footpath to a T-junction of paths.

2. Turn right along the edge of a field to a stile. Cross the stile and follow the clear path across a field to another stile. Cross this to reach the road. (If you wanted to avoid the stiles, you would take the road out of the village to this point.)

3. Turn left and then immediately right along a broad track, the drove. Follow this track between hedges and through the edge of a wood, eventually curving round to the right with a field to the left and the wood to the right. Continue uphill to reach a metalled farm track.

4. Turn right here and then left along a well-made lane. Pass to the left of some outbuildings and just before the drive of a house, turn right down a lane, turning into a fenced path just to the right of an outbuilding.

5. Go on down through the edge of woods and along the edge of a field. It can be a bit overgrown in summer. Look out for the nettles. You will eventually reach the road.

6. Turn right here and walk into the village returning to the start.

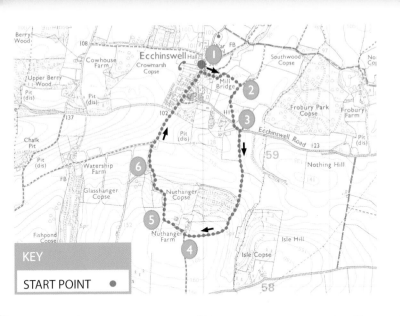

KEY

START POINT   ●

WINCHFIELD

FOR LOVERS OF WALKS BY WATER, TAKE A STROLL ALONG A LONG LOOP OF PEACEFUL CANAL AND THEN WALK BY A LAKE TO RE-JOIN THE CANAL.

The building of the Basingstoke Canal was completed in 1794. It ran for 37 miles (60km) from Basingstoke to the River Wey at West Byfleet with twenty-nine locks and a 1,200-yard tunnel at Greywell (see the Odiham walk, no. 3). Its purpose was to join rural Hampshire to London, carrying agricultural produce to the capital. The wars with the French of that period proved  commercially beneficial for the canal, as goods which would previously have been carried through the Channel were re-routed, more safely, by canal. However, the railway building of the 19th century rendered the canal unprofitable by the middle of the century. A series of owners tried to make it viable and military transport, during the First World War, briefly revived it. But after the war it declined and all attempts to revive it failed because of the cost of upkeep. By the middle of the 20th century, the canal was derelict.

Parts of the canal beyond the Greywell Tunnel had already been sold for development, when a group of enthusiasts started the campaign to restore it. The turning point came when the canal burst its banks at Farnborough and at Aldershot in 1968 and it was realised that benign neglect was not an option. To be safe it must be restored or destroyed. Hampshire and Surrey County Councils compulsorily purchased it in 1974 and restoration began. The work was a collaboration between the councils and the volunteers of the Canal Society and it was finally re-opened from Greywell to West Byfleet in 1991. It seems unlikely that the remaining five miles beyond the tunnel, known as the 'last five miles', will ever be re-opened. The tunnel collapsed in 1932, became completely impassable by the 1950s and is now home to a colony of bats, which are a protected species.

There are few boats on the canal in comparison with other canals, partly because as a Site of Special Scientific Interest the number of boats is restricted in order to preserve the wildlife and partly because it is connected to the wider network at only one point. However, for the walker this quiet backwater is a world of peace and tranquillity, disturbed only by the fluttering of the waterbirds on the water and the songbirds in the trees.

THE BASICS

Distance: 3¾ miles / 6km

Gradient: Flat

Severity: Easy

Approx. time to walk: 1½ hours

Stiles: None

Map: OS Explorer 144 (Basingstoke)

Path description: Canal towpath, country tracks, lanes and footpaths

Start point: Car park at Winchfield Hurst (GR SU 777537)

Parking: Parking in Sprats Hatch Lane opposite the Barley Mow (free) (RG27 8DE)

Dog friendly: Yes, but keep on leads where indicated by signage

Toilets: No public toilets on the walk

Nearest food: The Barley Mow Inn at the start

WINCHFIELD WALK

1. Exit the car park onto the canal and turn left. Continue along the canal towpath. You will pass a winding hole, used to turn narrow boats, a couple of kilometre posts and then a brick-built pillbox, built by the pioneer corps in 1940 just before the Battle of Britain. Not long after this you will arrive at a brick-built bridge. Leave the towpath here and head up to the bridge.

2. Turn right over the bridge, keep ahead to go through a white gate then turn right onto a broad track heading towards Tundry Pond. A sign near the gate states 'Dogs on leads' for this part of the walk. Follow the track as it turns left along the water's edge, then when you reach another brick bridge at the end of the pond turn left.

3. Go through a kissing gate beside a footpath finger post and head along a broad drive towards a former mansion house that is now the Four Seasons Hotel, Hampshire. In a few hundred yards, just before a cattle grid turn right onto another broad lane. In another couple of hundred yards bear right onto a footpath running between two fences. At its end go through a kissing gate then turn left onto a bridleway.

4. This is initially a broad gravel drive. When it bends right keep ahead on a grassy track that eventually narrows to a footpath. When that reaches a bridge cross over then turn right to go down to the canal towpath and continue along it.

5. From here it is a simple stroll along the towpath going under three bridges. When you go under the last, The Barley Mow Bridge, turn left off the towpath back into the car park.

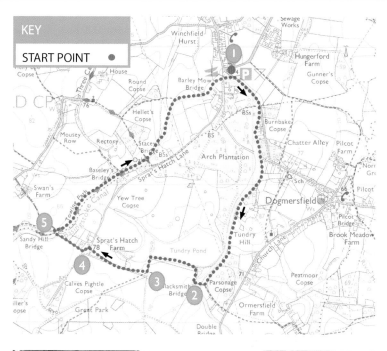

KEY

START POINT •

ODIHAM

King John and Magna Carta, the father of parliamentary representation, a former plague house and two picturesque villages linked by the Basingstoke Canal.

The octagonal keep of Odiham Castle was once dressed with stone, surrounded by a circular moat and high banking with rectangular moats providing further protection for the inner and outer baileys. King John had this castle built between 1207 and 1214 and although it was designed to be impregnable John used it mainly as a hunting lodge.

He was not a popular king and fell out with everyone including the French, the Church and particularly the barons. He levied heavy taxes on them and they turned to the French king for support. The barons occupied London and forced John to negotiate as an alternative to civil war. On 10 June 1215 he rode from Odiham Castle to Runnymede and agreed to the barons' demands. Despite this some barons rose against John and called on the King of France to invade and in 1216 they laid siege to Odiham for two weeks until the defenders surrendered. The French were amazed to find only thirteen men present. In late 1216 John died of dysentery and forces loyal to his son Henry II defeated the French and the rebels in 1217.

Henry had Odiham repaired and in 1236 gifted it to his widowed sister, Eleanor of Pembrokeshire. She then married the French nobleman Simon de Montfort, later the

6th Earl of Leicester, generally regarded as the father of parliamentary representation. In 1265 he led the second barons' revolt against a Plantagenet monarch. He was killed at the Battle of Evesham by forces led by the future King Edward I.

Various monarchs repaired and added to Odiham and in the mid-14th century King David II of Scotland spent three years there as a prisoner of war. Thereafter it was used variously as a prison and a hunting lodge but by the middle of the 15th century it was a ruin, its stone dressing plundered for new buildings and only the flint core remaining.

In the village of Odiham Jane Austen would recognise the bow-fronted former shop windows as the dressmaker's, milliner's and haberdasher's of her day. Look out for a former baker's shop and a couple of former inns.

THE BASICS

Distance: 5¾ miles / 9.2km
Gradient: One gentle slope
Severity: Easy
Approx. time to walk: 3 hours
Stiles: Four
Map: OS Explorer 144 (Basingstoke)
Path description: Canal towpath, fields and roads
Start point: Car park at Colt Hill (GR SU 748516)
Parking: Car park at Colt Hill, Odiham (free) (RG29 1AL)
Dog friendly: Yes, if they can manage stiles
Toilets: At Odiham on the route
Nearest food: Pubs at Odiham and Greywell

1. From the car park, make your way to the canal towpath and turn right along it. Continue along the winding towpath, passing a footbridge, a road bridge and a lift bridge. You will see Odiham Castle on the right, through the trees. Ignore the first two or three entrances because access that way is  prevented by a ditch, which is in fact the remains of the castle moat. You will soon come to a clearly signposted entrance with information boards.

2. When you have seen enough at the castle, exit the grounds and turn right to continue to the end of the navigable part of the canal. You will pass the last winding hole, then some buoys to prevent boats going any further and then you come to the Greywell Tunnel, which is now home to a healthy colony of bats.

3. Go up the path at the side and then over the top of the tunnel, turn right and then left onto the road through Greywell. Pass the Fox and Goose or stop off for refreshment and then continue through Greywell to the entrance to the church at a lychgate.

4. Go through the gate to the left of the lychgate and go to have a look at the church. Then turn left through a gate opposite the church and go straight ahead across a field. The path has changed from the current OS Map: you cross the stile ahead before veering right to another stile. Cross that and follow a path to a bridge, which is back to the marked OS path. Go through a kissing gate and follow the path to another kissing gate ahead.

5. From here go gently uphill, straight across a clear path through a crop field, to a road. Cross the road and go into a large field. Turn left on a clear path along the edge of the field into the next smaller field and go diagonally across it and through an opening into another crop field.

6. Go straight across on a clear path to an opening, concealed until you are almost there, onto another road. Cross the road diagonally to a stile into a field. Follow the line, pointed by the footpath fingerpost, veering right across the field to a stile. Turn right into a narrow path between hedges, which emerges at the road.

7. Turn left along the road and continue until you reach Recreation Road on the right. Turn right and then quickly left to go along the edge of the recreation field. Go along a narrow lane between houses, cross a road and continue on this lane to reach the church. You can go through the churchyard to the right of the church to

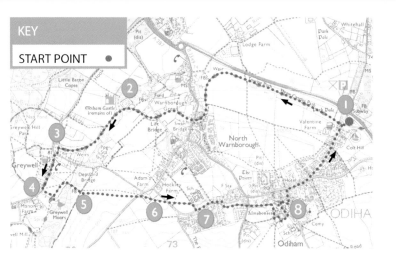

find the Pest House and at the back the almshouses. The Pest House is a remnant from the time of the Plague when sufferers were given shelter there. Then exit the churchyard and turn right. Just along the road on the right is the Bridewell, which is now the library but was a prison.

8. Fork left and then left again to reach the High Street, passing the public toilets on the way. Turn right into the High Street and continue to a fork, where you go left. When you reach the bridge over the canal, cross it and turn down to the towpath and return to the car park.

GRAYSHOTT

INDUSTRIAL ARCHAEOLOGY, THE AUTHOR OF *LARK RISE TO CANDLEFORD* AND A POEM BY ALFRED, LORD TENNYSON ALL FEATURE ON THIS DELIGHTFUL WALK.

The three artificial lakes that lie on the edge of Ludshott Common were created, according to local tradition, as 'hammer ponds' for use in the iron production industry. No one knows for certain when they were built but this was part of a famous iron-making area from the 16th to the 18th centuries. However, there is no archaeological evidence to show that the ponds were ever used in the iron-making process. In fact they were probably fishponds. You can still fish here for carp, roach and trout and the ponds have become a rich habitat for a variety of wildlife. The place is teeming with ducks and they are obviously used to humans, as they will paddle en masse towards you, expecting to be fed. There are other delights to look out for like the iridescent kingfisher as it flits along the water's edge looking for lunch and the grey wagtail. Take a couple of pocket field guides, as the entire area is a Site of Special Scientific Interest because of the wildlife.

The walk round the ponds and up across the common was a favourite of Flora Thompson, author of **Lark Rise to Candleford**. She wrote: 'One hot September afternoon near the

end of the last century a girl of about twenty walked without knowing it over the border into Hampshire from one of the neighbouring counties.'

She came to Grayshott in 1898 and worked in the post office there for two years. In her writings she mentions many of the landmarks and walking paths around the village. From the last of the ponds emerges Cooper's Stream, which runs eventually into the River Wey. But a short distance from the ponds it passes a house and there by the path you will find a wishing well that she was fond of and mentioned in her writing. Here you will also find beside it a plaque with a poem that Alfred, Lord Tennyson wrote in 1863.

Flower in the crannied wall,
I pluck you out of the crannies,
I hold you here, root and all, in my hand,
Little flower – but if I could understand,
What you are, root and all, and all in all,
I should know what God and Man is.

THE BASICS

Distance: 2 miles / 3.2km
Gradient: One long gentle ascent and one steeper descent
Severity: Easy
Approx. time to walk: 1¼ hours
Stiles: None
Map: OS Explorer 133 (Haslemere & Petersfield)
Path description: Woodland paths
Start point: Car park at Waggoners Wells (GR SU 862344)
Parking: Car park at Waggoners Wells (near GU26 6DT)
Dog friendly: Yes
Toilets: Headley Road car park in Grayshott
Nearest food: Pubs and cafes in Grayshott

GRAYSHOTT WALK

1. From the car park make your way to the edge of the first lake and turn left along it. At the end of the lake turn right across it and then left along the path on the other side. There is a waterside path along the second lake but it is eroded and blocked in parts, so keep to the higher path. However, there are several points where you can walk to the waterside path to get a view of the lake. At the end of the lake continue on the path to reach the third lake.

2. At the third lake, you can go down to the waterside path, which is in better condition. At the end of the lake go up some steps to reach the upper path and continue in the same direction through the wood, passing a bridge on the left. You will soon arrive at a house. There is a path to the right just before the house. Ignore the path and go on passing to the left of the house. Almost immediately you will see a well to the right of the path.

3. Continue on the path, passing another bridge to the left and keeping right at a fork. The path continues gently uphill to reach a multi-path junction.

4. Take the nearest right path. Almost immediately you come to a crossroads of paths and continue ahead. Keep on this path through the woods as it becomes a leaf-covered path by a long mossy bank and descends towards the lakes.

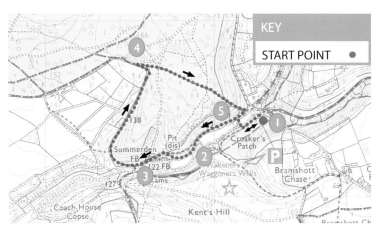

5. Near the bottom, take the right fork to reach the forest road and turn right to go back to where you crossed the lake on the outward path. Re-trace your path across the end of the lake to the car park. Afterwards you can explore the pretty village of Grayshott and visit the building that contained the post office where Flora Thompson worked. It's two buildings away from the current post office and marked with a plaque. In The Avenue is a house called The Ferns. This is where she obtained lodgings when she could no longer bear to live in the post office. It was in her room there that she consigned her writing to the fire (see Walk 5).

LIPHOOK

Parts of this glorious walk through the woods and the downs so beloved by *Lark Rise to Candleford* author Flora Thompson and are almost unchanged since she knew it.

Flora Thompson was born Flora Timms in 1876 at Juniper Hill in Oxfordshire. Her father was a stonemason and her mother had been a nurserymaid. At the age of fourteen she became assistant to the postmistress Kezia Whitton, the model for the character Dorcas Lane in her best-known work, ***Lark Rise to Candleford***. Kezia was a strong, capable woman, in charge of the post office and the forge since the death of her husband. However, Flora admitted that she had based the character on several postmistresses she had known. ***Lark Rise***, although biographical, was written at Dartmouth in the 1930s and was clearly a fictionalised account of her own story.

She came to Liphook in 1916, when her husband was appointed postmaster, but she already knew and loved the area from her days as a young assistant sub-postmistress at nearby Grayshott (see Walk 4). She was impressed by the famous writers who used her post office at Grayshott, including George Bernard Shaw and Arthur Conan Doyle. Overawed by their brilliant conversations, she burned all her own writings.

By the time she returned as a mature married woman with children, she was writing again and having her work published. She wrote ***The Peverel Papers*** as a regular contribution to ***The Catholic Fireside***. Weavers' Down became Peverel Down, where she described her long country walks. Although the first part of this walk is much altered and built upon, as you continue into the woodland and downs on sandy sunken paths it remains much as Flora would have known it. You can stop at a wide sandy viewpoint that Flora described, in her 1925 guide to Liphook, as 'a perfect panorama of beauty. Forestmere Lake lies like a mirror in the woods directly beneath; to the south is the blue ridge of the South Downs; to the north the heathery heights of Hindhead.' As you walk across the downs and through the light and airy birch forest, you may be as fascinated as Flora was by the countless tracks walked by previous generations, 'most of them overgrown and deserted.'

As you return to the start, consider Woolmer Gate, the first house the Thompsons bought. Although she only lived here for two years, it was her dream location, right at the edge of her beloved Peverel Down.

THE BASICS

Distance: 3¾ miles / 6km

Gradient: Gentle

Severity: Moderate

Approx. time to walk: 2 hours

Stiles: None

Map: OS Explorer 133 (Haselmere and Petersfield)

Path description: Pavement, lanes, tracks and woodland footpaths

Parking: At the end of a cul-de-sac at Pines Road just off Longmoor Road

Start point: Cul-de-sac on Pines Road (GR SU 820317)

Parking: At the end of a cul-de-sac at Pines Road just off Longmoor Road near the A3 junction (GU30 7PL)

Dog friendly: Yes

Toilets: None on route

Nearest food: The Deers Hut pub on the route

LIPHOOK WALK

1. From where the car is parked, at the end of a cul-de-sac continue along the footpath passing Woolmer Gate on your right. This was the first house that Flora Thompson and her husband ever owned and they bought it new.

2. Then turn right towards the Deers Hut public house and when you reach it, turn right again along the road in front of it. Keep ahead on this ignoring a way-marked junction on your left (this is the return route). At the next junction on your left leave the road and bear left onto the way-marked Shipwrights' Way.

3. Keep on this broad, roughly surfaced lane, passing a hotel complex on the right and then a golf course. When you reach a paths crossroad keep ahead on the well-marked Shipwrights' Way. Then go through a metal gate. This is part of a military training area and signs warn you not to pick up any objects. In a few hundred yards you will emerge from the wood and have a great panoramic view over the downs. At a path junction turn left through the metal gate and head downhill on a narrow sandy footpath.

4. At the first junction keep ahead then bear right at the next junction. The path now curves right to enter a wood and follows the edge of it.

5. When the path forks, keep left then turn left again in a further few yards to go onto a broad flat path through the woods. After it narrows it will reach a junction by an old way-marker post. Keep ahead in the same direction. This is a public bridleway and soon you will pass a finger post on your left confirming this.

6. Keep ahead through the next paths crossroads, then, when it forks, bear right to pass another finger-posted junction. Then keep ahead as you pass a cottage on the right that is just visible through the trees.

7. When the path forks again at a multiple bridleway fingerpost, keep right and continue through the woods on a fairly firm path. When this ends at a metalled lane turn left onto it to join the Shipwrights' Way. Keep on this to reach the junction by the Deers Hut then turn right. You will probably be in need of refreshment so head in. Then re-trace your steps to the start.

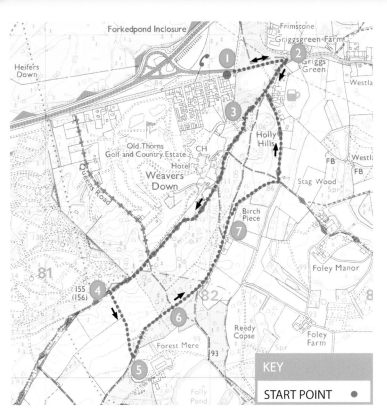

KEY

START POINT ●

SILCHESTER

EXPLORE THE REMAINS OF A ROMAN TOWN, A MUCH OLDER IRON AGE SETTLEMENT AND A PARISH CHURCH DATING BACK TO THE 12TH CENTURY.

Calleva Atrebatum was a substantial town that was developed on the site of a much older Iron Age settlement, from the mid-first century AD. The Roman builders laid out a regular street grid, which you may be lucky to see if conditions are right. It had a forum, public baths, a travellers' rest house and an amphitheatre. Archaeologists have identified several small temples and there may also have been a Christian church. The remains of the walls, built around the year 270, are among the best preserved in England. While the dressed flint and stone exterior has long vanished, the core with its round stones and lime mortar shows how it was constructed. Seven gates provided passage through the walls. Of these only four remain including those at the north and south and at the amphitheatre.

When the Romans left Britain in the 5th century many of their towns were still occupied, but not Silchester. It appears to have been abandoned between 550 and 650. It is recorded as Silcestre in the Domesday Book of 1086. Archaeologists have concluded that the medieval village occupied the ground between the amphitheatre and south gate but the only sign of its existence is the Church of St Mary the Virgin that dates from the 12th century and is contained within the Roman Walls. As a sacred site this is much older as there are two temples under the church and its yard. The church is magnificent and has an early 16th-century rood screen, which survived the Reformation and the Civil War because it was removed and hidden. It was rediscovered in the 1860s and restored. The village was probably abandoned near the end of the 14th century, around the time of the Black Death. Modern Silchester, which lies to the west of the Roman remains, dates from the early 17th century.

The Roman amphitheatre was built on the eastern edge of the town and consisted of earth walls enclosed by wood. The earth was also used to form circular terraces. It could accommodate up to seven thousand spectators who would gather to watch gladiators' combat, wild beasts fighting each other and public executions. By the 3rd century the construction had been altered with the walls re-built in stone.

THE BASICS

Distance: 3¼ miles / 5.2km

Gradient: Flat

Severity: Easy

Approx. time to walk: 1¾ hours

Stiles: None

Map: OS Explorer 159 (Reading)

Path description: Broad gravel track, footpaths and country lanes

Start point: Car park at Calleva Roman Town (GR SU 635628)

Parking: At the English Heritage Car Park for Calleva Roman Town (RG7 2HP)

Dog friendly: Yes

Toilets: None on the route

Nearest food: The 17th-century Red Lion at Mortimer West End (RG7 2HU) or the Calleva Arms in Silchester

SILCHESTER WALK

1. Head into the corner of the car park near three pillars. Then continue along a wide gravel path with a fence on the right and trees on the left. Through gaps on your left you will see the walls and ditch of the earlier settlement. Just after the path turns left there is a junction, by a kissing gate and footpath finger post. Pass this and keep ahead towards the Roman walls now visible in front of you. Keep on the path and follow it through a gate. Then it turns right and left to reach the walls.

2. Turn right onto a broad gravel track that goes anti-clockwise round the walls. When this bends right look out for two kissing gates on your left and turn left through the second.

3. Then follow a leafy footpath beside the walls. There are a few sections of exposed wall on your left as you walk along, allowing you the opportunity to see how they were built. Look out also for the defensive ditch on your right. Eventually the path leaves the woodland and continues by the wall with the entire wall visible on your left. Only the core with its lime mortar is left but originally it would have been faced with hammer-dressed flint.

4. When you reach the south entrance gate to the town turn left through it then turn right and climb up on top of the walls to continue your journey. You can now look out over the area once occupied by the town and see how big it was. Eventually the path will come to a gate. Go through this into the churchyard, then visit the church.

5. After you have visited the church turn right out of the door, right at a path junction then left onto Church Lane. Follow this past The Old Manor House on the left and a junction on the right. At the next junction where the road turns left into Wall Lane go through a kissing gate on the corner to visit the remains of the amphitheatre. You can walk through it and up and around the broad banking. Then continue along the field to exit through a gate back onto Wall Lane. Turn right along it and in a short distance turn left to go through a gate onto the Silchester Trail. Almost immediately go through a kissing gate onto the Roman Walls and turn right. Walk around the walls to pass the North Gate then, when the path turns left, look to your left over the fields. After a period of dry weather and if the light is right you can see the old grid lines of the Roman streets. When you finally reach a gate go through it then turn right onto the path back to the car park.

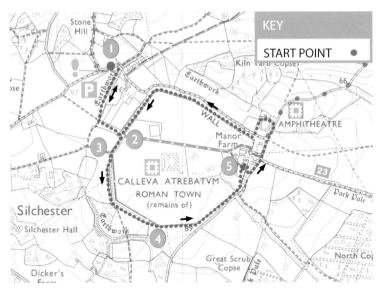

CHAWTON

WALK IN JANE AUSTEN'S FOOTSTEPS IN THE LOVELY COUNTRYSIDE AROUND HER LAST HOME.

Jane Austen came to Chawton in 1809 and spent the last eight years of her life here. Those years were her most productive and all of her novels were published in that time. *Sense and Sensibility*, *Pride and Prejudice* and *Northanger Abbey* had been finished much earlier but she reworked them in the Chawton years. She loved Hampshire and was dismayed when her father retired to Bath from the rectory at Steventon in 1800. In the years at Bath and then, after her father's death, at Southampton, she barely wrote at all. Then her brother Edward gave her the opportunity to return to the countryside she loved and a comfortable and spacious home. He had inherited the large estates of Chawton in Hampshire and Godmersham in Kent. When the cottage became vacant, he offered it to his mother and sisters rent-free for life. She wrote:

Our Chawton home, how much we find
Already in it to our mind;
And how convinced that when complete
It will all other houses beat.

In the house you can see the tiny table, next to the window, which she used for writing.

When she was well Jane walked all around the area and much of this walk she would recognise, through woodlands and across fields. She writes frequently in her correspondence of visiting the Great House, the home of her brother. She would also have attended the Church of St Nicholas, where her mother and sister are buried, but the previous church and not the current Victorian one. She also wrote of walking to Farringdon, to accompany her friend Harriet home: 'the plan is that we should all walk with her to drink tea at Farringdon'. Harriet was the eldest daughter of John Benn, who was rector at All Saints, Farringdon for sixty years from 1797 until 1857. All Saints Church is still much the same. There are also houses in the village that she would have known including the 17th-century Holly Cottage and Cruck Cottage.

She would certainly not recognise Massey's Folly, the large, complicated red-brick building, which dominates the centre of the village. It was built by Thomas Massey, John Benn's successor as rector. Neither would she have known the disused railway line of the return journey, since the railway age was yet to dawn when Jane Austen died.

THE BASICS

Distance: 4¾ miles / 7.6km

Gradient: Some gentle slopes

Severity: Easy

Approx. time to walk: 2½ hours

Stiles: Six

Map: OS Explorer 133 (Haslemere and Petersfield)

Path description: Field and woodland paths, disused railway track

Start point: Car park opposite Jane Austen's House (GR SU 708375)

Parking: Car park opposite Jane Austen's House at Chawton (GU34 1SB)

Dog friendly: Yes, if they can manage stiles

Toilets: None on route

Nearest food: Cassandra's Cup next to car park

CHAWTON WALK

1. Exit the car park opposite Jane Austen's House and turn left to go along the pavement running beside the road signposted to St Nicholas Church and Chawton House. Pass a footpath sign opposite Ferney Close but keep ahead. This is the return route. Then pass the drive to Home Farm on your left. The next drive on your left is the entrance to Chawton House and the parish church of St Nicholas. Both may be visited after the walk.

2. In the meantime continue ahead to pass a barrier and go along a lane. When this ends, bear left onto a narrow footpath then go over a stile and along a much wider tree-lined footpath. Dogs can squeeze through the wire fence at the stile easily. Cross a second stile. At the third stile you emerge from the woods. Cross this and turn left in the direction indicated by the finger post. Follow a faint but visible path over pastures. At the other end of this cross a stile and continue on a well-surfaced track through another strip of woodland. Exit this and continue on the track through crop fields. This rises gently and continues into woodland where a sign advises you that dogs should be kept on leads. Then the track heads downhill. Come out of the woods to reach a T-junction.

3. Turn left to pass some buildings then turn right towards the former village hall, an ornate brick-built construction. Turn left into the churchyard, visit the church and note the two ancient yew trees that are considerably older than the church. Then leave the churchyard by the other path, turn left to pass some pretty cottages and then when you reach the former village hall, Massey's Folly, turn right and then left opposite a footpath finger post. At a T-junction turn right and then left at the next crossroads. Walk along this lane to reach a main road. Carefully cross it then continue along a lane that runs to the right of Farringdon Cottage.

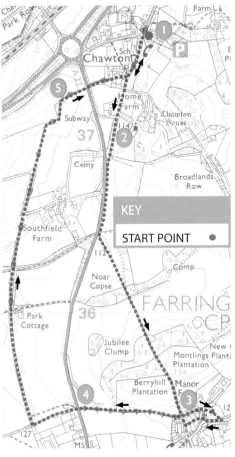

4. Follow this to reach an old railway bridge then turn right at a footpath sign just before it. Go down some steps then follow the path left to get onto the old trackbed and continue along it. Keep ahead at a crossroads then again when you reach a junction to the right. Go under the railway bridge here. When the track bends left keep ahead on a footpath running along the left-hand side of crop fields. When the path turns right near a way-marker keep on it. Then in a short distance turn left at another way-marker and follow the path through woodland.

5. At the end of the woods turn right at another way-marker and keep on the narrow path that runs gently downhill to go through a kissing gate and down some steps to the main road. Cross this carefully then go up more steps and across a stile before continuing on the path. Cross one last stile then walk the short distance down Ferney Close before turning left to re-join your outward route.

Silchester

Chawton

Burley

BURLEY

An Iron Age fort, a dragon slayer, witches and some wicked fudge.

Burley is a picturesque little village but behind the prettiness there be dragons and witches. Granted the dragon is long gone, slain by a knight back when knights offered that sort of service. But there are still witches and a couple of shops selling the paraphernalia to conjure up the odd spell. One is the famous Coven of Witches, named in the 1950s by Britain's then most famous witch, Sybil Leek. She roamed the streets of Burley with a jackdaw on her shoulder and claimed to be the successor to the Black Magician Aleister Crowley. However, the succession of journalists and crowds of people visiting upset some of the inhabitants and eventually her landlord asked her to leave so she moved to America. Her successor is Julie Forest who describes herself as a 'fully initiated New Forest Witch'. You could try one of her witchcraft courses for beginners or you could just sample the wickedly delicious Burley Fudge from the Burley Fudge Shop.

There are other ancient traditions in Burley. Villagers still practise commoning and retain the right to graze their animals in the forest. Cattle and ponies can be found wandering about the streets, and even the fire station has a cattle grid. The open heathland and woodland, bog and grassland on this walk provide a rich habitat for a variety of wildlife. Some of the creatures will be difficult to spot but you will certainly see the grey squirrels flashing from tree to tree everywhere.

High up on Castle Hill you will find the remains of an Iron Age fort. It's an earthwork consisting of a single rampart surrounded by a ditch and although it has been cut into by various tracks and is covered in vegetation and trees you can still make out the shape of the rampart and get a clear view across the heathland from the top. Legend has it that this was once the home of a fierce dragon. Various versions of the tale exist though none of them end happily for the dragon. There's an early 17th-century scroll, which claims that Sir Maurice Berkeley, Lord of the Manor, killed it but died shortly thereafter himself. Whether from injuries sustained in the fight or not no one knows but the feat is immortalised in the name of the pub at Brook, the Green Dragon.

THE BASICS

Distance: 3¾ miles / 6km

Gradient: A few gentle climbs and descents

Severity: Easy

Approx. time to walk: 2 hours

Stiles: One

Map: OS Explorer OL 22 (New Forest)

Path description: Woodland paths, gravel tracks and road

Start point: Car park in Burley (GR SU 211031)

Parking: Pay and display car park at Burley (BH24 4AB)

Dog friendly: Yes, if they can manage stiles

Toilets: At car park

Nearest food: The Queens Head and many other pubs and cafés in Burley

BURLEY WALK

1. From the car park head through the mall to the road, cross the road to the pavement and turn right. Go down the road for about 400 yards and look for a footpath sign to Burley Street, going off to the right. Cross the road and take the footpath. The footpath goes alongside the road, gradually climbing above it and then descending to the road again. When you return to the road, cross to the pavement and turn right along the road briefly, looking for the entrance to Burley Hill House. Turn in here to the left.

2. Go through the gate to the right of the main gate and continue along a path between two fences. This winds along the side of fields and through woodland and past a path crossroads until eventually it arrives at a stile.

3. Cross the stile and turn right onto the gravel lane. Go up here until you come to the fort. You will see a short steep rise in the road and when you look to the sides, you can see the ramparts. Continue up and enjoy the views from the wide plateau of Castle Hill. You can see the ramparts all round and the shape of the moat in places.

4. When you have seen enough turn back along the road that you came on. When you reach the stile, go straight ahead and continue down the gravel road, passing Burley Beacon. The names of the houses will let you know when you are there. There is Burley Beacon and Beacon Cottage. After that you will arrive at the road.

5. Cross the road and go on in the same direction along a grassy path and then through the woods until at the edge of the woods you come to a clear track. Turn left along this track until it meets a broad track.

6. Turn left along the track and when you reach some buildings pass to the right of them onto a broad gravel track. When it joins a metalled road, continue in the same direction to a crossroads with a gravel road. Cross the gravel road and take the footpath ahead to the road. Cross the road and turn left down to the car park.

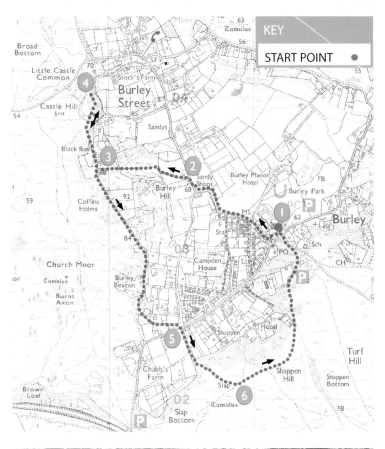

KEY

START POINT •

NORTH POULNER

THIS WALK TAKES YOU THROUGH THE VARIED HABITATS OF THE NEW FOREST, BY RIVER, WOODLAND AND MOOR AND TELLS THE TALE OF A GOOD DEED WITH FATAL CONSEQUENCES.

Birdsong in the hedges and woodlands and squawks from the lakes will be your accompaniment throughout this walk. At the start, listen carefully for the sound of the woodpecker. You may be lucky enough to see one but you are very likely to hear one, chipping away at a tree. Look out for the sudden blue flash of the kingfisher, which haunts the lake just beyond the trees here. A tinier blue flash across the green of the nettles or teasels is likely to be a dragonfly.

As you walk on around the lakes, access is quite restricted in order to protect the wildlife, but you will see plenty of waterbirds. If you see a duck with her ducklings, she will swiftly have them halfway across the lake if you make a sound. These are not tame park birds, used to humans, and they will treat any intruder with suspicion. Before you leave the lakes behind, you will pass the Spinnakers Sailing Club. Unfortunately it is a private club for members only apart from occasional open days and tasters, so you can only watch the sailing. Likewise the fishing that allows anglers close to the water's edge is fishing club only with no day passes.

As the walk continues alongside the Avon River, you reach the Alice Lisle pub. This is named for Dame Alice Lisle, who lived at Moyles Court Manor, which you will pass shortly. It is now a school but in 1685 Dame Alice lived here. She was seventy at the time and gave shelter to two members of Monmouth's defeated army, who were fleeing from the Battle of Sedgemoor. She was arrested, charged with treason and tried at the 'Bloody Assize' of the infamous Judge Jeffreys. The jury, believing her story that she would give shelter to anyone in need, found her innocent three times but Jeffreys bullied a guilty verdict from them and sentenced her to be burned alive. James II would not pardon her but conceded that she should be

beheaded rather than burned. She was executed in Market Lane in Winchester, where a plaque marks the spot. She was the first of many and the only woman to be condemned in the killing spree which followed.

THE BASICS

Distance: 4½ miles / 7.2km

Gradient: Mostly flat except for one section where the gradient is moderate

Severity: Moderate

Approx. time to walk: 2¼ hours

Stiles: None

Map: OS Explorer OL22 (New Forest)

Path description: Tracks, lanes and footpaths

Start point: Car park at New Poulton Lakes (GR SU 157067)

Parking: Car park at New Poulton Lakes (free) (BH24 1SB)

Dog friendly: Yes

Toilets: None on route

Nearest food: Alice Lisle Pub on the route

1. Leave the car park and take a footpath that runs to the left of an interpretation board and reserve map. Keep left where the path forks and follow it along a wide grassy track. When you reach a junction by a dog poo bin turn left and continue through woodland with a stream to your left to reach a signposted crossroads.

2. Turn left here and go across the bridge then turn left onto footpath 19, walking along beside a tall wire fence with a lake beyond. Turn right at the end of the fence onto a way-marked path that follows the fence round the end of the lake.

3. When you reach a kissing gate go through it, turn right onto a lane then left to go through another kissing gate onto a footpath just beyond Mistletoe Cottage. Follow this past another lake (unfenced). When you reach a kissing gate at the end go through and turn right.

4. Pass the Spinnaker Sailing Club on your right and continue on a broad track that is signposted as the Avon Valley Path. Shortly turn left at a bridleway sign and continue on the Avon Valley Path as it runs to the left of another sailing club. When you come to the end of this path go through a gate and emerge onto a road beside Ivy Cottage. Turn left onto the road, keep ahead to pass a cattle grid then turn left towards The Alice Lisle. Pass this delightful country inn and continue to a road junction opposite a thatched cottage. Then turn left through a gate and continue along the Avon Valley Path.

5. When you reach the next junction turn right to go through a gate onto a road. Cross the road and continue on the path that runs beside the road to Linwood. Pass Moyles Court School on your left then cross the road at the next junction, keep right towards Linwood then almost immediately turn right onto a track that runs beside Rockford Common and to the right of a lane that heads uphill to the car park. Pass between two pretty thatched cottages and then Chatley Wood House. From here the track heads uphill into the woods. Keep ahead as it reaches the top of the hill and passes a cottage on your right. Just past this is a junction but keep ahead on the broad track ignoring all junctions until you reach a point where the track splits at a three-way junction. Then keep left.

6. When you reach a crossroads at Foxglove Corner, keep ahead to pass a cottage and the track to Deer Cottage, then continue on a broad track. Keep ahead

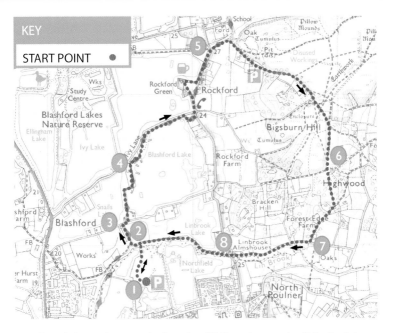

through the next crossroads, then downhill through a wood until the track bears right a gate. Go through it and continue downhill on a footpath.

7. At a T-junction beside Linbrook Thatch turn right onto a lane. Follow this to a T-junction, cross the road and turn right. Shortly turn left onto a footpath.

8. Follow this through the woods with the lake on your right. Just after you reach the second lake turn left to cross the footbridge then right onto a footpath at the opposite end and follow your outward route back to the car park.

BROCKENHURST

HOUSES WITH CATTLE GRIDS, THOUSANDS OF ANTS, BOMB
CRATERS AND ANCIENT WOODLANDS TO SUPPLY THE TIMBER
TO BUILD WARSHIPS.

The Woodland Inclosures are areas of open land, which have been enclosed for the
purpose of producing timber, and many date back to the 18th century. Various Acts of
Parliament were needed to legalise the process including the New Forest Acts of 1698,
1808, 1877 and 1949.

Woodland Inclosures were first set aside for silviculture at varying dates: Parkhill and
Pignall in 1751; Stubby Copse in 1829 and Pignalhill in 1846. Originally created to supply
timber for warships for the Royal Navy they now exist in perpetuity. Verderers' Inclosures,
under the 1949 Act, must be open to stock grazing for most of the time and are held on
150-year leases. Where they were previously intensely forested, mainly with conifers, the
Forestry Commission is now restoring the inclosures to heathland and mire.

In the middle of the 19th century Josiah Parkes, a noted expert in drainage, built the
Victoria Brick and Tile Works in the forest. Its main purpose was to manufacture tile-pipes
to drain below-surface water into special cuts and thus turn boggy ground into productive
agricultural land. The tile works produced the first mass-produced pipes, creating a boom
in drainage projects. The New Forest was at the forefront of this boom, funded by the
Southampton and Dorchester Railway Company in return for access over forest land. You
can still see the drainage cuts, which support a wide variety of wildlife, but the factory
is long gone and all that remains is Victoria Tilery Cottage, the former works manager's
house. There are several schemes now in place with the aim of turning drained land back
into wetlands to provide wildlife habitats.

As you walk through the forest look out
for bomb craters created by some of
the 2,700 bombs that were dropped in
the New Forest in World War II. You can
also spot lots of nests built by southern
wood or horse ants. They are mostly
found in coniferous forests and like the
sun so their nests are nearly always in

the open. Then there are the horses and cattle that graze on the common land of the
Forest. You will see them everywhere. They go along roads and into gardens to forage,
which is why you will see lots of houses with cattle grids in their drives.

THE BASICS

Distance: 3¾ miles / 6km

Gradient: Negligible

Severity: Easy

Approx. time to walk: 2 hours

Stiles: None

Map: OS Explorer OL22 (New Forest)

Path description: Forest roads and grassy paths

Start point: Balmer Lawn car park (GR SU 303031)

Parking: Balmer Lawn car park (SO42 7TS)

Dog friendly: Yes

Toilets: None on route

Nearest food: Balmer Lawn Hotel and others in Brockenhurst

BROCKENHURST WALK

1. From the car park walk out to the road and turn right. Go along the road until the road bends right and then continue ahead on a gravel path.

2. The gravel path continues straight, passing grazing horses and cows on the common to your left and Tilery Hill car park. At a fork go left to arrive at Standing Hat car park.

3. Go right here passing to the left of the buildings of Victoria Tilery Cottage. Continue on the forest road as it winds round, passing forest rides until you reach a cycle track crossroads marked 305. Just before that look to the left for several bomb craters under the trees.

4. Turn left here. Go straight along the forest road through a mainly conifer forest. Look out for anthills on either side of the path as you go. When you reach a gate, numbered 304, go through and continue to reach shortly another gate on the left.

5. Go through the gate and take the left fork along a grassy ride. When the ride meets a gravel forest road, continue ahead on the forest road. This will bring you back to a gate to Standing Hat car park. From here re-trace your outward journey to Balmer Lawn car park.

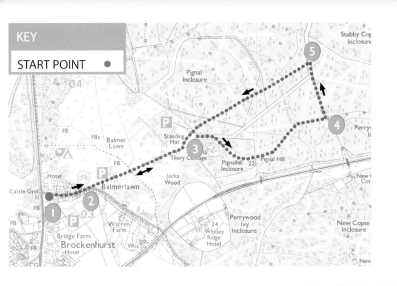

KEY

START POINT ●

NETHER WALLOP

Possibly the most picturesque village in Hampshire, Nether Wallop's thatched houses, adorned with roses and fronted by cottage gardens, were used for location shots in the BBC TV Series of Agatha Christie's *Miss Marple*, starring Joan Hickson. You will pass Jane Marple's house, Dane Cottage, on the walk. It's in Five Bells Lane, which was used in the series along with several other lanes.

But there's more here than a fictional sleuth. This is one of several Wallops that lie along the course of the Wallop Brook, where watercress production was once an important part of the economy. The beds disappeared in the late 1970s but the plant still grows wild.

The Square was once the thriving heart of the village. It had a general store and two grocers, one including the post office. The Trout off licence was an ale house, which brewed its own beer and had a shed in the front garden where a local man made cricket bats by hand from local willow. The legendary W.G. Grace used one of these. The proprietor of the post office doubled up as the village baker and produced smoked bacon in a small shed behind his shop. Lastly there was a butcher with a small slaughterhouse at the rear and a curing shed for making bacon. It closed in 1971.

The village's Endowed School was founded in 1838 and once had three teachers and 120 pupils while the village mill has a new lease of life as a fishing business. You can cross a ford known as the Splash and nearby Dancing Green Cottage recalls a time when villagers danced around the maypole on the village green.

One of the oldest parts of the village is St Andrew's Church. The part now forming the choir stalls was once the chancel of the original Saxon Church. Opposite the front is an unusual pyramid-shaped memorial covering the burial vault of Dr Francis Douce, who died in 1760. Its design is based on Egyptian funerary monuments and Douce left precise instructions for its construction and how it was to be aligned to the meridian. He was apparently obsessed with the preservation of his body and the afterlife. According to local lore the good doctor is still occasionally seen wearing a cutaway blue coat and yellow pantaloons, walking round the pyramid swinging his cane.

THE BASICS

Distance: 2 miles / 3.2km

Gradient: A couple of very gentle climbs

Severity: Easy

Approx. time to walk: 1¼ hours

Stiles: None

Map: OS Explorer 131 (Romsey, Andover and Test Valley)

Path description: Lanes and well-surfaced footpaths

Start point: St Andrews Church Nether Wallop (GR SU 303364)

Parking: At St Andrews Church Nether Wallop (SO20 8ET) (but not when there is a service taking place please)

Dog friendly: Yes

Toilets: None on route

Nearest food: The George Inn, Middle Wallop. (The Five Bells was closed at the time of writing but may have re-opened.)

1. Head downhill from the church and along Church Lane. Pass the post office and keep left to pass between Rose Cottage and The Old Forge. Then pass the Wesleyan Chapel on your left just before turning right at the junction with Church Hill. Keep ahead along High Street passing several picture postcard cottages.

2. At the T-junction, the cottage opposite and slightly to your right is Dane Cottage, which featured as Miss Marple's cottage home in St Mary Mead in the TV series. Turn left to pass The Five Bells, then head uphill passing Beech Cottage and the Great Barn. When you reach a thatched cottage on your left called Rags Corner, turn right into Ducks Lane and proceed downhill. Then head uphill to pass Wallop House before turning right at a junction into Five Bells Lane.

3. At the end of this cross a ford, or take the bridge, to reach the village green. Then turn left and keep ahead on The Causeway and cross a bridge to reach a T-junction opposite the entrance to the Manor. Turn right into Heathman Street.

4. Head along this road, passing the junction on the right that would take you back to The Square and the post office. On your left here is the Old Post Office. Continue past the old school building on your right then keep right where the road bends opposite a junction on the left to Dene Farm. Pass between Place Farm House and Place Barns then, shortly after passing the entrance to Nether Wallop Mill, turn right onto a footpath.

5. Cross a footbridge where you will have a great view of the mill on your right. Then continue along a well-maintained grassy footpath. When you reach a footbridge cross it to enter the churchyard. Visit the church then continue through the churchyard to return to the start.

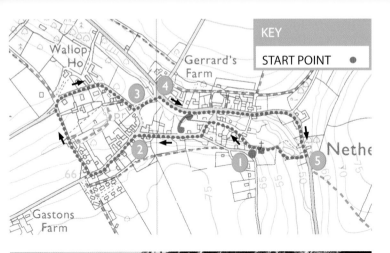

KEY

START POINT •

ROMSEY

INSPECTOR WEXFORD, LORD PALMERSTON, THE ODD WATER VOLE AND A NORMAN CATHEDRAL ARE ALL ENCOUNTERED ON THIS WALK.

Romsey is a pretty market town situated on the River Test but throughout the 1980s and 90s it doubled as the fictional Kingsmarkham in the TV series *The Ruth Rendell Mysteries*, which featured George Baker as Inspector Reg Wexford, her genial detective. In the original stories the town is in Sussex but the company that produced the series was based in Hampshire and so Romsey was chosen as the location for filming. The layout was a close match to Rendell's descriptions so several buildings including The Corn Exchange and the Norman Abbey will forever be associated with Kingsmarkham by those who followed the series.

The abbey sits on a site that has been Christian for over 1,100 years. Inside you can still see the remnants of the older Saxon church. Amazingly it survived the dissolution of the monasteries because four 'Guardians' petitioned Henry VIII and bought the church for £100. Worth seeing are the Norman and Early English arches that were erected between 1120 and 1250 and the Saxon roods, one from the year 960 inside St Anne's Chapel and the other from the 11th century on an outside wall.

The Broadlands Pew in the Abbey was used by the owners of the stately home on the edge of the town. In 1736 the estate was bought by Henry Temple, the first Lord Palmerston. His descendant the third Lord Palmerston was a famous prime minister during the reign of Queen Victoria. During the Crimean War he was a great supporter of Florence Nightingale, who was a neighbour of his from Embley Park. She is buried in St Margaret's Church at East Wellow. Palmerston died in 1865 and is remembered locally by his statue, which stands in Market Place.

The Romsey Barge Canal that forms a large part of this walk was completed in 1794 to link the town with Redbridge and Andover. It fell out of use within fifty years and closed in 1859 after which a large part of it was built over for the railway. Its locks have gone and with it the ability to maintain the water level and so it now looks more like a small stream. It is a wonderful wildlife habitat and if you are lucky you may see water voles, the odd kingfisher or a rare otter.

iStock

THE BASICS

Distance: 4¾ miles / 7.6km

Gradient: Negligible

Severity: Easy

Approx. time to walk: 2 hours

Stiles: None

Map: OS Explorer 131 (Romsey, Andover and Test Valley)

Path description: Streets, canal path and footpaths

Start point: Tourist Information Centre (GR SU 351212)

Parking: Several pay and display car parks in the town (SO51 8BT)

Dog friendly: Yes

Toilets: In Bell Street

Nearest food: Many cafés and pubs in Romsey

ROMSEY WALK

1. Go to the left of the Tourist Information Centre towards King John's House and walk through the garden. Continue from the garden, through a car park and exit the car park through a black gate. When you reach Latimer Street turn left towards the station.

2. Follow Latimer Street as it becomes Station Road and crosses Malmesbury Road. Ahead you will see a tunnel under the railway. Go through the tunnel.

3. Follow the lane ahead between hedges until at a bridge it reaches the canal. Go along the canal, passing three more footbridges and going under a road bridge. Continue along the canal passing another bridge until you reach a crossroads of paths.

4. Turn left here and follow the footpath through woodland and meadow until it reaches Fishlake Stream. Turn left along the stream to the bridge, cross the bridge and continue along the stream and lake on the other side until the path emerges at a drive. Turn right to the main road.

5. At the road turn left and follow the road back towards Romsey. Before you reach the railway, turn left into an industrial estate. The road crosses the stream and then there is a footpath sign to the right. In high summer the path alongside the stream can be a bit overgrown, so watch out for nettles, but it is a clear path, which is obviously used. It soon emerges onto a broad grassy bank. This path continues to Duttons Road.

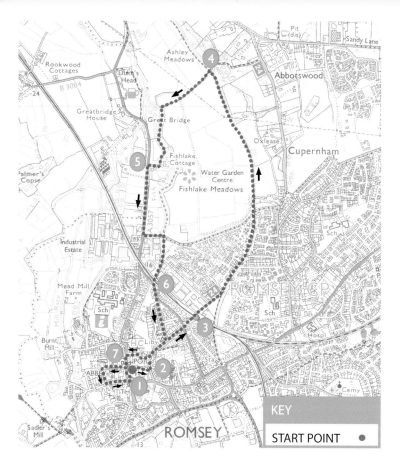

KEY

START POINT ●

6. Turn left along Duttons Road and follow it to re-join Station Road. Turn right and go along onto Latimer Street. Look out for Lortemore Place on the right. Turn right and continue to the end of the street, where you can go through Abbey Walk to reach Church Street.

7. Turn left towards the Tourist Information Centre, but cross the street to the abbey and have a look at it. Walk all the way round to the street called The Abbey and along it to the Market Place, where there is a statue of Lord Palmerston. Have a look at the Cornmarket to the right and then go back along Church Street to the start of the walk.

SOUTHAMPTON

The *Titanic*, ancient city walls and Jane Austen all feature in this city walk.

One of the worst maritime disasters in history was the sinking of the RMS *Titanic*. This 'unsinkable' vessel set sail from Southampton on its maiden voyage to New York on 10 April 1912. Four days later it hit an iceberg and sank. It now lies on the seabed over two miles below. Fifteen hundred people died in the disaster and they are remembered today because of a series of books and films, most notably James Cameron's *Titanic*, from 1997, starring Leonardo DiCaprio and Kate Winslet.

You will pass many of the buildings associated with the ship, the first being Canute Chambers, the former offices of the White Star Line, owners of *Titanic*. A plaque on the gatepost tells you that this is where anxious relatives gathered for news of family and friends. Of the crew some 724 were from this area and the final death toll was 549.

South Western House, which you pass next, was where the first-class passengers stayed the night before embarking. It had its own railway station and they would get off the train at the hotel then board it again in the morning to travel the last few hundred yards to the *Titanic* berth. There is a brief background shot of the hotel in the film. Apparently the grand staircase on Titanic was modelled on its main staircase.

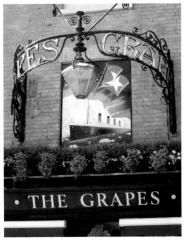

The White Star tavern in Oxford Street was the Alliance Hotel in 1912 and housed some third-class passengers, including a family from Devon and their neighbour. The family perished but the neighbour made it and lived out her life in Connecticut. Opposite it is the Grapes pub where the stokers and engine room workers drank. Some of them cut it a bit fine for the voyage and, running back to the docks, they were cut off by a train. As a result they missed the boat but their companions, who ran in front of the train, made it. Another pub you will encounter later in the walk is the Platform, frequented by dockers and sailors. James McGrady, a first-class steward and the last body recovered from the sea, had given his address as The Platform. This is the pub in the film where DiCaprio's character, Jack Dawson, wins his ticket for the voyage in a poker game.

THE BASICS

Distance: 3¾ miles / 6km

Gradient: Flat

Severity: Easy

Approx. time to walk: 2 hours

Stiles: None

Map: OS Explorer OL22 (New Forest)

Path description: Pavements, city walls and lanes

Start point: Ocean Village, Southampton (GR SU 426108)

Parking: At Ocean Village (SO14 3TL) (several options – charges apply)

Dog friendly: Yes but keep on a lead

Toilets: In Bargate Street

Nearest food: Many establishments passed on the walk

1. From the car park head back along the road past Enterprise House, Admirals' Quay and a Tesco Express to reach a T-junction.

2. Turn left along Canute Road to reach Canute Chambers, former offices of the White Star Line. Then continue to a railway crossing across the street from the former South Western House hotel and Southampton Docks Railway Station.

3. Turn right and cross the road to walk along Terminus Terrace to turn left into Oxford Street.

4. Pass the Grapes pub on the left and opposite it the White Star Tavern, formerly the Alliance Hotel.

5. Turn left into Latimer Street, then cross into Queen's Park, and go right to reach the memorial to General Gordon of Khartoum. Continue right and out of the park to cross onto Briton Street, then along it to a T-junction, then turn right into High Street.

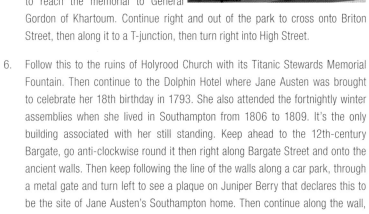

6. Follow this to the ruins of Holyrood Church with its Titanic Stewards Memorial Fountain. Then continue to the Dolphin Hotel where Jane Austen was brought to celebrate her 18th birthday in 1793. She also attended the fortnightly winter assemblies when she lived in Southampton from 1806 to 1809. It's the only building associated with her still standing. Keep ahead to the 12th-century Bargate, go anti-clockwise round it then right along Bargate Street and onto the ancient walls. Then keep following the line of the walls along a car park, through a metal gate and turn left to see a plaque on Juniper Berry that declares this to be the site of Jane Austen's Southampton home. Then continue along the wall, through another gate, down some stairs and turn left to follow the outside of the wall. Pass the remains of the Castle Garderobe Tower then the arcades before turning left into Blue Anchor Lane.

7. Go past the Tudor House Museum, where the ghost of Anne Boleyn allegedly walks, and enter St Michael's Church, the oldest building still in use in the city. Inside

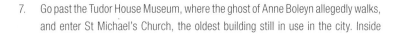

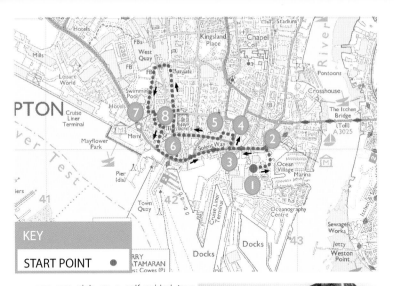

you can pick up a self-guided tour leaflet. Return to the Tudor House, turn left then left again at the Duke of Wellington Pub, then keep ahead to pass the Medieval Merchant's House.

8. Turn right into French Street and proceed to a T-junction, then turn left into Canute Street passing the Watergate, another part of the ancient walls, the Platform tavern and the medieval God's House, a 13th-century tower that was once the entrance to the town from the quay. Subsequently it was the town gaol and later an archaeology museum. A bit further on the right is a large red-brick building, Admiralty House. Once the main post office for the docks it gathered all overseas mail that went go on board the RMS (Royal Mail Ship) *Titanic*. Post office staff were employed on the liner, sorting the mail during the sea crossing, and several died when she sank. Next door is the Docks, Gate 4, the *Titanic* berth, and just to the left through the gate is the Titanic Memorial. It's not open to the public but if you ask one of the security guards nicely they may let you have a quick look. Then continue along Canute Street to return to the start.

The 10th anniversary celebrations of the Cunard liner QEII

The quay at Lymington

BOTLEY

A COUNTRY PARK WITH WOODS, FARMLAND AND A RIVER AS WELL AS THE HISTORIC MANOR FARM, LOCATION OF THE TV SERIES *WARTIME FARM.*

Manor Farm Country Park lies on the banks of the River Hamble near the village of Botley. The old village, mentioned in the Domesday Book, was closer to Manor Farm, and the former parish church, St Bartholomew's, lies just beyond the farm buildings. Completed in the 13th century, it was until 1836 the main centre of worship. However, as the village grew and moved north, it no longer had the

capacity for the population and it was too far away across fields and stiles. So a new church was erected to the west of the village and named All Saints and the old church was re-named St Bartholomew's. A tree fell on it near the end of the 18th century leaving only the chancel undamaged. The ruins were cleared away and a new wall was built leaving a much smaller church.

Manor Farm has been a farm for more than six centuries. For the BBC TV Series **Wartime Farm**, historian Ruth Goodman and archaeologists Peter Ginn and Alex Langlands endeavoured to re-create a typical English farm, as it would have been run during the years of World War II. This was the third period of historical farming that they had investigated. Starting with a Victorian farm in 2009, they farmed at Acton Scott in Shropshire for a year. Then in 2010 they moved forward to the Edwardian age at Morwhellham Quay in Devon. Both locations were working historical farms that are outdoor museums.

Manor Farm is part of a country park. Entrance to the park and grounds is free although there is a charge for parking. While there's an admission fee to enter the farm itself it is not essential to the walk. But if you have children on this walk there is lots to amuse them inside. Actors play the part of the farmer, his wife and servants and you can see her cooking in the excellent farmhouse kitchen, washing clothes by hand and beating carpets. There are lots of cute animals to pet and seed can be bought to feed the chickens, guinea fowl and ducks. Every afternoon they have a 'meet the animals' session, where kids can get close to rabbits, chicks and ducklings and even have a go at hand-milking a cow.

THE BASICS

Distance: 2½ miles / 4km

Gradient: Sight gradients

Severity: Easy

Approx. time to walk: 1½ hours

Stiles: One, easily managed by all dogs

Map: OS Explorer OL22 (New Forest) and 119 (Meon Valley)

Path description: Forest paths and farm tracks

Start point: Barnfield car park (GR SU 498110)

Parking: Barnfield car park (charges apply) (near SO31 1BH)

Dog friendly: Yes

Toilets: At Barnfield car park

Nearest food: At kiosk in car park and there's a cafe at Manor Farm

BOTLEY WALK

1. Leave the car park and go across the play area, veering left at the swings. Then head towards the corner of the woods and onto a footpath that runs beside a noticeboard. Keep ahead at the first crossroads, then turn right at a junction, then immediately left at the next junction. At the next junction on the left keep ahead then at the following junction turn sharp left, head downhill, then turn right, continue downhill then turn left and go down some steps before turning left onto the way-marked Hamble Valley Strawberry Trail. You could also divert for a short while by turning right to go down more steps to a small beach at the river's edge.

2. Enjoy this pleasant woodland footpath. At a junction turn right past a way-marker and head downhill on some steps. Then cross a footbridge and go back uphill on more steps. Next go through a barrier and keep ahead through the woods as indicated by the way-marker. On you right you can see the river through the trees.

3. When you reach a flat wooden bridge just in front of a path junction take the left-hand path that heads uphill away from the river's edge. When this path reaches a T-junction with another path, turn right.

4. Keep on the main path, ignoring all junctions. Then go down some steps, cross a bridge and a low stile before continuing uphill past a Strawberry Trail way-marker. In case of doubt after you go through a clearing it's the broad path on the left that you take. The path emerges from the woods and keeps going straight ahead with a hay meadow on your right and hedgerow to your left.

5. At the end of this meadow turn left at a crossroads to go through a gate then continue with the hedgerow on your right-hand side. When you reach a gate at the end of the path go through it. Keep ahead then turn right if you want to visit Manor Farm. Otherwise turn immediately left onto a broad footpath that is still the Strawberry Trail and head along it. When you reach a gate it's time to part company with the Strawberry Trail, pass a barrier and keep ahead on the same broad path, passing a signpost to Barnfield. Keep on this path until you see the picnic and play area through the trees to your right. You can take any path right to get onto it and then return to your car or keep going to reach the crossroads you passed through when entering the woods at the start of the walk and re-trace your steps from there.

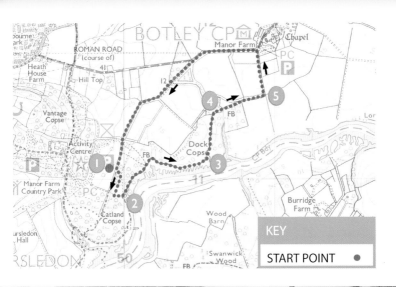

KEY

START POINT ●

LYMINGTON

W ALK THROUGH A NATURE RESERVE THAT WAS ONCE
E NGLAND'S LARGEST SALT PRODUCER AND LEARN ABOUT
BOAT BUILDING AND SMUGGLING.

From the Middle Ages salt production was the main wealth creator on this part of the coast. Throughout the 18th century this was the biggest sea salt industry in England with a continuous line of works from the town to Hurst Spit. Some of these salt pans or salterns are now the mudflats, ponds and ditches of Normandy Lagoon which is part of the Keyhaven Nature Reserve and provides a rich and varied habitat for a variety of species.

Once these salterns would have looked very different and you would have seen evaporating ponds and boiling houses as well as windmills for pumping water and docks for transporting the salt. The industry declined as sea salt was replaced by mined salt from Cheshire, which was much cheaper to produce. The last working saltern in Lymington closed in 1865.

Fortunately this was not the only local industry. Boats were being built over the same period. In the late 13th early 14th centuries, during the reign of King Edward I, the shipyard at Lymington built nine ships for the Royal Navy. The Berthon Boat Company that you pass on the walk has been building boats here since 1877 but there has been a boatyard on this spot since the 16th century. The warships are long gone but there are yachts, of all shapes and sizes, moored at pontoons in the town's three marinas. Being on the Solent and close to the Isle of Wight makes Lymington a very popular sailing centre.

Where you have boats you will find smuggling. In the latter half of the 17th century this was another economic mainstay involving brandy, silks, coffee and particularly tea, which

suffered from high levels of taxation. Local boat owners acquired these goods tax-free across the Channel then landed them in the many creeks around Lymington, where they were loaded onto carts or packhorses and moved quickly inland for onward distribution. Local legends tell of High Street cellars, interconnected by tunnels, being used to store the contraband and of churches where it was almost impossible to worship because the box pews and pulpit were jammed full of smuggled goods. There was considerable local support for smuggling because the high taxation priced the goods out of the reach of all but the very rich.

THE BASICS

Distance: 5 miles / 8km
Gradient: Mostly flat
Severity: Easy
Approx. time to walk: 2½ hours
Stiles: None
Map: OS Explorer OL22 (New Forest)
Path description: Hard-surfaced footpaths, country lanes, pavements
Start point: Bath Road Car Park (GR SZ 332951)
Parking: Bath Road Car Park (SO41 3SE) (charges apply)
Dog friendly: Yes but keep on a lead where requested
Toilets: At car park
Nearest food: Many food outlets on the walk

LYMINGTON WALK

1. From the car park head past the toilets and the lifeboat station towards the marina. When you reach the path alongside the marina, turn right along it. Pass the Sea Water Baths on your right and continue along the marina. When you come to a broad road, then a junction, turn right, with the marina to your left and walk along it to a car park.

2. Go through the car park and exit at a gate to the left at the end. Take the path to the left to walk out round the sea walls. Continue on along this path with the salterns to your right and the Solent to your left. The path turns to right and left around the salterns. Pass one footpath on the right and then at Eight Acre Pond turn right.

3. Go along the edge of the pond away from the Solent and emerge at a road. Turn right and then right again onto Normandy Lane. Follow this long, winding country lane to a T-junction.

4. Cross the road, veering slightly left into Broad Lane. This becomes Church Lane and continues to a T-junction with the High Street, passing the Wavy Wall on your left. This section is early 19th century, possibly built by Hanoverian soldiers. These walls are built like this to give extra strength to the single-brick construction. There's another section of wall on your right before reaching the one mentioned above. It was built by the author Dennis Wheatley when he lived at the now demolished Grove Place.

5. Just before you turn right into the High Street stop and look at the house on your left. This is Monmouth House, built in the early 17th century and the oldest complete domestic house in Lymington. Now head along the High Street. Buildings of interest inlcude the parish church of St Thomas on the left-hand side of the road. Parts

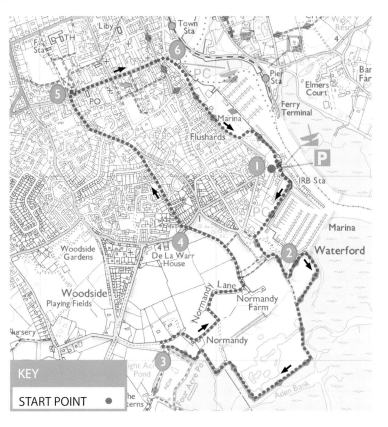

of it date back to 1250. On the right-hand side, fronted on the street by railings, is Bellevue House, which was built in 1765 and was the home of Charles St Barbe who was a saltern owner, banker and five times the local mayor. Just past this on the right take the time to have a look down Ashley Lane. This passageway has been in existence since 1335 and you will see a plaque on one of the walls declaring that Admiral Arthur Phillip lived there in the late 18th century. He sailed on the first fleet to the new penal colony that would become Sydney and became the first Governor of New South Wales.

6. On the left look for the Angel Inn, an 18th-century coaching Inn. The town's proclamations would be announced from the balcony here. Just after this, before the main road turns left, continue ahead into the cobbled Quay Hill, which then turns right into Quay Street, which emerges at The Quay.

7. Walk ahead along The Quay and on into Bath Road. Continue along Bath Road until you see an entrance to the park on your left, just opposite Solent Avenue. Go through the park, past the bandstand to return to the car park.

BOLDRE

THIS SHORT WALK BY LEAFY LANES RECALLS THE JOURNEYS AROUND HIS PARISH OF THE 18TH-CENTURY POLYMATH REVEREND WILLIAM GILPIN.

When William Gilpin became the vicar at the church of St John in 1777, it was in a parlous state. The parish at that time included Brockenhurst, Lymington and Beaulieu and Gilpin set about improving both the fabric of the buildings and the condition of the people. As you walk the lanes around the church, you are following in Gilpin's footsteps as he visited every parishioner. These lanes, albeit narrower and dirtier, would have been very familiar to him. He got to know what they needed and realised that education was crucial. He sold some of his paintings and writings to raise a fund to build and maintain a school, with twenty places for girls and twenty places for boys, to serve the children of the labouring classes.

He was an experienced and innovative teacher, having been the headmaster at Cheam School for many years, where he introduced new teaching methods and encouraged the boys to think for themselves rather than learn by rote. He was also more concerned about moral development than academic progress: 'It is my wish to improve their sense, and if possible, to add judgement.'

He obviously succeeded in the case of William Mitford, his ex-pupil, who was responsible for offering him the living of Boldre, no doubt realising that his gifted teacher would improve the parish as he had Cheam School. Having built the school, Gilpin went on to alleviate the lot of the most impoverished by improving the poor house. He offered to put up money for repairs but the parishioners responded by raising money to build a new one. Gilpin wrote about the new house and compassionate conditions, which were also more economical. His account was widely circulated as a model for the running of poor houses.

However, Gilpin was best known at the time for his writings about art. He was one of the mainstays of the picturesque school of landscape painting, maintaining that to make a scene 'picturesque' generally required some re-arranging of the composition by the artist: 'A pillared frontage is beautiful, but to make it picturesque it must be in ruin.'

He even suggested that 'a mallet judiciously used' would make Tintern Abbey more picturesque, which may have contributed to his being satirised by Jane Austen and others.

WILLIAM GILPIN, M.A.

VICAR OF BOLDRE DURING THIRTY YEARS,
AND PREBENDARY OF SALISBURY,
BORN AT SCALEBY CASTLE, NEAR CARLISLE, A.D. 1724,
DIED AT BOLDRE, APRIL 5TH 1804,
A MAN EMINENT FOR THE ACCOMPLISHMENTS OF HIS MIND,
THE PURITY OF HIS HEART,
AND THE EXCELLENCE AND SIMPLICITY OF HIS LIFE.

In grateful Remembrance
of his faithful Administration of the Pastoral Office,
and of his Munificence
as the Founder of the School in this Parish
for the Education of the Children of the Day Labourers of Boldre,
his Friends and Parishioners
dedicate this Monument to his Memory.

THE BASICS

Distance: 2¼ miles / 3.6km

Gradient: Several moderate climbs and descents

Severity: Easy

Approx. time to walk: 1¼ hours

Stiles: None

Map: OS Explorer OL 22 (New Forest)

Path description: Footpaths, lanes and road

Start point: Car park in Boldre (GR SZ 324993)

Parking: Behind Boldre Church – but not during services please (SO41 5PG)

Dog friendly: Yes

Toilets: None on route

Nearest food: Red Lion in Boldre (on route)

BOLDRE WALK

1. From the car park go into the churchyard then turn left and go clockwise round the perimeter. Turn left to go through a gate onto the lane in front of the church then bear left to pass the car park entrance and along a lane. At the top of a hill with a bridle path on the left and a footpath on the right turn right.

2. Follow this broad, well-surfaced footpath downhill, past Hollins Nursery, to reach a T-junction then turn left onto a lane.

3. Keep on this lane to the next T-junction, then turn right to cross Boldre Bridge and enter the village. Keep on this street to reach the Red Lion, on your left, then turn right into Royden Lane heading in the direction of Sandy Down.

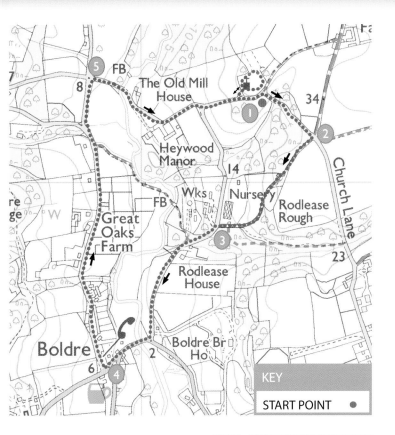

4. Pass through the village and keep ahead to reach a junction at Lower Sandy Down, then bear right.

5. When you reach a crossroads turn right onto Church Lane and follow this back to the church, keeping ahead as you pass a junction to the right. Before returning to the car park, visit the church and churchyard, where you can find Gilpin's tomb at the back just a few yards from a notice directing you to it.

BROOK

TAKE THIS WALK THROUGH OAK WOODLANDS, BY PRETTY
COTTAGES, STREAMS AND FORDS AND CONSIDER A HISTORIC
TALE OF DEATH BY ACCIDENT OR DESIGN.

The walk starts at the Rufus Stone in the heart of the
New Forest. The stone has now been replaced by a
metal pillar retaining the original wording. William II,
known as Rufus, because of his high colouring, was
killed here by an arrow, shot by Sir Walter Tyrrell, which
allegedly bounced off an oak tree. Sir Walter and all the
witnesses fled the scene, leaving the king's body to be
unceremoniously loaded into a cart and transported to
Winchester by a woodsman, named Purkiss. You can see
the route he took on the opposite side of the road from
the stone, heading into the woods.

However, the first identification of this spot was not made until 1745, when the stone was
raised, supposedly where the fateful oak tree grew. So it may have happened elsewhere
in the New Forest; for example, Beaulieu has been suggested. It is certainly true that Sir
Walter Tyrrell fled to France, while William's brother, Henry, swiftly claimed the throne and
had himself crowned at Westminster within days.

William was killed while out hunting and the New Forest was actually fairly new at the time,
having been designated as the king's hunting ground by his father, William the Conqueror.
It was recorded in the Domesday Book of 1086 as the Nova Foresta. The word forest
did not have the meaning of woodland at that time, but of hunting ground. The penalties
for encroaching on the king's hunting ground were severe, including death or mutilation.
However, by way of compensation, limited commoners' rights were granted to the people
to pasture animals on the land. Even now the ponies and cattle that you see everywhere
within the New Forest belong to the commoners, although their numbers and rights have
diminished over the centuries.

There are six rights still attached to ownership of certain properties. The main right is of
pasture, which allows commoners to 'depasture' their ponies in the forest. Others, less
used, are the right to pasture sheep, the right to fuelwood, and the right of common mast,
which allows their pigs to eat acorns and beech nuts. No longer used at all are the right to
common marl, to collect lime from clay pits, and the right of turbary, to cut peats for fuel.

THE BASICS

Distance: 3½ miles / 5.6km

Gradient: Very gentle

Severity: Easy

Approx. time to walk: 1½ hours

Stiles: None

Map: OS Explorer OL22 (New Forest)

Path description: Lanes and bridleways

Start point: Rufus Stone Car Park (GR SU 270125)

Parking: Rufus Stone Car Park (near SO43 7HE)

Dog friendly: Very; and dogs are most welcome in the Sir Walter Tyrrell Inn

Toilets: No public toilets locally

Nearest food: The Sir Walter Tyrell, The Bell Inn and The Green Dragon are all passed on the walk

BROOK WALK

1. From the car park cross the lane to look at the Rufus Stone. Then walk back towards the lane and turn left to go in the direction signposted to the Sir Walter Tyrrell Inn. Pass the inn, with its beer garden, well-equipped children's play area and sign saying 'Dogs Welcome', then continue on the lane. Pass North Barn on the left then Canterton Manor Farm on the right. At a junction on the right, by a small red post box, bear left. After the next building on the right, Keeper's Cottage, cross a ford or take the bridge depending on the water level, then pass Blackthorne's Farm on the left.

2. At the next house on the left the road bends to the right to pass Skers Farm and then enters the village of Brook. Follow the lane through the village to a T-junction opposite The Bell Inn then turn right onto the B3079 towards Cadnam.

3. Continue on the roadside path passing a Victorian post box and then the Green Dragon, a pretty thatched inn serving good food and real ales. Then cross a footbridge, and pass a footpath on your left just before Cedar Cottage. Next cross a drive beside Canterton Lodge, on the right, to bear right onto Canterton Lane which passes Rose Cottage.

4. When the lane ends besides a large house keep ahead onto a gravel-surfaced bridleway. Just after the next house on the right turn right onto another bridleway. Pass Twin Oaks cottage on your left then follow the broad track of the bridleway into beautiful woods. This is boggy in places but it soon emerges from the woods and continues as a well-surfaced path. Follow it to a T-junction beside the red post box you passed earlier.

5. Turn left onto the lane and return to the start of the walk.

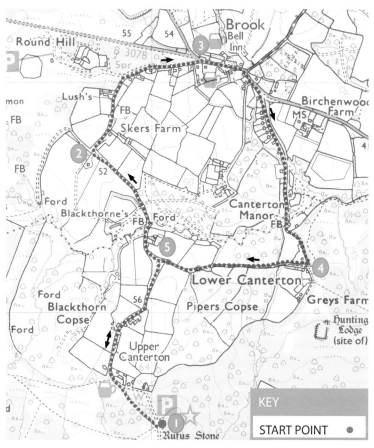

KEY

START POINT ●

ALRESFORD

Start from the station, whether you park here or arrive by train. The walk along Broad Street takes you back to a bygone age. The buildings are mainly Georgian and would have been here when Jane Austen walked this street, popping into some of the lovely bow-fronted shops for ribbons, muslin or millinery. The town here is actually New Alresford, which originated around 1200. Old Alresford is to the north of Alresford  Pond, created by Bishop de Lucy in the 13th century. The pond still supplies the watercress meadows, which are sustained by the perfect natural environment of plentiful, clear, fast-flowing streams. Until the 1970s the watercress used to be transported to London and beyond on the Watercress Line, which is now run as a heritage railway by a team of volunteers.

If you can, do this walk on a day when the trains are running. There are various locomotives, including steam trains, and the carriages are from different eras of rail travel, including first-class carriages, a buffet car and an elegant dining car. Even if you don't take the train, have a look at the station, where the volunteers in their authentic railway uniforms keep everything as it would have been, from the waiting rooms to the signs and vintage posters.

The clear waters of the River Alre also supported the woollen industry and you will pass two mills on the walk. The first is the town mill at the bottom of Mill Hill. It is an ancient site but the building that you see is 19th century. It was latterly converted to a laundry, which also provided hot baths for the locals with the waste water. This area was also the centre of the tanning trade, where the skins would be scraped and tanned and made into leather. The atmosphere would have been putrid with the stench of decaying meat, urine and noxious chemicals. Further along the river the 13th-century fulling mill is now a beautifully renovated private home. It would once have harnessed the power of the river to drive the hammers which beat and tightened the woollen cloth, and the din of the hammering would have filled the air. The rural past was not the idyllic backwater we see today, but was often noisy and smelly.

THE BASICS

Distance: 3½ miles / 5.6km

Gradient: A couple of moderate climbs and descents

Severity: Moderate

Approx. time to walk: 1¾ hours

Stiles: None

Map: OS Explorer 132 (Winchester)

Path description: Pavements, well-surfaced footpaths and lanes

Start point: The station car park (GR SU 588324)

Parking: Alresford Station Car Park (SO24 9JG) (charges apply)

Dog friendly: Yes

Toilets: At the railway station and in Station Road

Nearest food: Several good eating places in Broad Street

ALRESFORD WALK

1. Leave the station car park and head along Station Road. Just before you reach the public toilets on the left, bear right onto a footpath, which will take you into the churchyard. Keep left towards the entrance of the church then pass it and keep left to exit the churchyard and reach a T-junction with West Street.

2. Cross the road and continue along Broad Street. Cross to the right side of the street, then turn right along The Soke, then turn right again onto a drive beside Pond View Cottage to reach the Old Pond. Trace your route back from here to Broad Street, cross it, then turn right to go down Mill Hill. Ladywell Lane is on your left and you turn along it. But before doing so head further down Mill Hill to have a look at the old town mill on the right.

3. At the end of Ladywell Lane continue on a footpath to reach the banks of the River Alre and turn left. Walk along the waterside, passing the Memorial Gardens and the Old Fulling Mill. When the water ends beside River View Cottages turn right towards the Eel House.

4. Follow this path past a recreation ground to arrive at the Eel House. It was used to catch eels in traps and an interpretation board explains its history. Continue past it, turn right over a short bridge, then left to continue on the path on the opposite side of the water. Shortly after the bridge, the path veers away from the river to ascend gently beside a wooden fence and then along a tree-lined section. When it ends at a gate, keep ahead to cross a narrow lane and continue on a footpath, which has trees on the left and a field on the right.

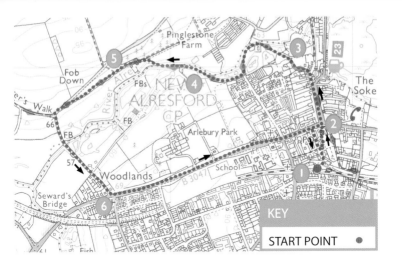

5. At the end of the path continue along Drove Lane following it round to the left opposite a junction, then continue along it to its end.

6. At the T-junction turn left into The Avenue, pass the old Toll House and continue along a broad, tree-lined path that was once the main road. Then enter the town and keep ahead to reach Station Road on the right. Turn into it and follow it back to the start.

ALTON

Stroll around the town where Jane Austen shopped and where Sweet Fanny Adams was born.

Alton is the town closest to Chawton, where Jane Austen lived for the latter part of her life. Although considerably changed, there are parts of the High Street that she would recognise. In 1811 she visited Newman, the Apothecary and Surgeon, at his home in 74 High Street, while a little further along at 31–33 is The Swan Hotel, from which she took the coach to London. Number 10 was the site of the bank, where her brother was a partner, and her friend Rebecca Parker

Terry lived at number 1. Jane wrote about dining there with her when she had just been widowed. Just across the street at number 4 lived William Curtis, Jane's doctor, whom she affectionately called her 'Alton Apothecary'.

Jane would have known of the Battle of Alton in 1643, when Oliver Cromwell's Parliamentarians attacked a group of Royalists, forcing them into St Lawrence's Church. Have a look at the west doors of the church for the musket holes. But she would have known nothing of Sweet Fanny Adams, who was born in 1859 after Jane died. The initials SFA, often believed to stand for some rather ruder words, are actually short for Sweet Fanny Adams who was brutally murdered here on 24 August 1867. She and two friends were walking along Tanhouse Lane when they met Fredrick Baker, a local clerk. He gave the friends money to buy sweets and a halfpenny to Fanny to walk with him to Shalden a couple of miles further on. Fanny took the money but refused to go with him. So he lifted her up and vanished with her into the hop fields. When her friends arrived home and told Fanny's mother what had happened, neighbours organised a search party and found her mutilated body. Baker was arrested and charged. He pled innocence and then insanity but was found guilty and became one of the last felons to be publicly hanged outside Winchester Gaol.

Two years later the Royal Navy introduced tinned mutton as sailors' rations. They called the meagre rations 'Sweet Fanny Adams' after some wag suggested part of her remains had ended up in the Navy victualling station. Through time its usage changed to mean 'absolutely nothing'.

THE BASICS

Distance: 2½ miles / 4km

Gradient: Negligible

Severity: Easy

Approx. time to walk: 1 hour

Stiles: None

Map: OS Explorer 144 (Basingstoke)

Path description: Town streets and park

Start point: Alton Station or the car park (GR SU 722397)

Parking: Station or various car parks on the route; car parking is expensive on weekdays (GU34 2PY)

Dog friendly: Not a lot of open space

Toilets: At car parks

Nearest food: Many pubs and cafés on the route

1. From the station car park turn left along Paper Mill Lane and go under the railway bridge. Continue up the hill to Ashdell Road and turn right along it. Turn right shortly onto a path to King's Pond. Walk almost all the way round the pond and emerge onto the road further along.

2. Turn right along the road, go under another railway bridge and walk past the brewery on the right to a mini-roundabout.

3. Cross over onto the pedestrianised Turk Street, which takes you to the High Street. Turn briefly left and then right into Westbridge Walk. Go through the Mall to the Market Square. (Lady Park Place car park is just next to the Market Square if you want to start from here.)

4. Pass the Town Hall and return to the High Street and turn left along it as far as the Assembly Rooms and the Curtis Museum on the right.

5. Turn left here into Church Street, pass some almshouses on the right and then you will reach the church on he left. Spend some time having a look at the church.

6. Then cross the road and go into Chauntsingers Road, follow the road as it bends to the left and turn right into Victoria Road (Victoria Road car park is another option to start from). At the T-junction with the main road turn left. Go along the main road to Paper Mill Lane and turn right to the station.

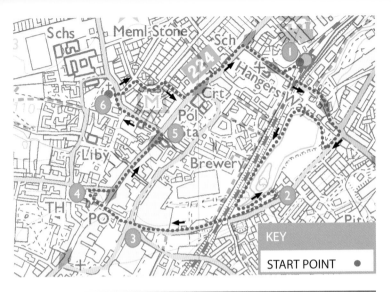

89

WINCHESTER

TAKE A WALK THROUGH HISTORY, WITH GARDENS, A HIGH STREET, A RIVER AND A MAGNIFICENT CATHEDRAL.

Winchester has been an important political and religious centre at various times in its history. The Romans had a large settlement here, but when they left the town declined until Alfred the Great made it his capital in the 9th century. His statue stands in the High Street, which takes the line of the old Roman Road.

Before that, just beside the 19th-century bridge over the River Itchen, the 18th-century city mill has been restored to working order. Then after the Abbey Gardens, you reach the elaborate Victorian Gothic Guildhall, which replaced the more modest building near the Buttercross, distinguished by the large hanging clock and a statue of Queen Anne. The 15th-century Buttercross, refurbished in the 19th century, was the spot where medieval country traders sold their goods.

At the end of the High Street the fortified 12th-century Westgate is now a museum. Just around the corner is the 13th-century Great Hall, which is all that remains of the castle. Go in to have a look at the round table. This is not the round table of Arthurian legend, but a 13th-century version, painted in Tudor times, with King Arthur represented by a young Henry VIII. Winchester is a walk through time but the undoubted star is Winchester Cathedral.

The massive edifice of the Norman cathedral, consecrated in 1093, was a statement of power and majesty to a conquered people. It was completely re-modelled in the 14th century by William of Wykeham in the Perpendicular Gothic style. However, the solid Norman pillars are still there beneath the soaring columns and the heavy round arches are visible in the North Transept. William of Wykeham too is still there, in his tomb. Look for his effigy in the Chantry Chapel in the nave. Many kings and bishops were buried in the cathedral, including St Swithun, whose tomb drew thousands of pilgrims over the years. However, the most visited grave today is that of Jane Austen, the novelist, who was buried here in 1817. The stone covering her grave makes no mention of her writings, but by the 1850s it was attracting so many literary pilgrims that the verger of the cathedral was heard to ask if 'there was anything particular about that lady; so many people want to know where she is buried.'

THE BASICS

Distance: 3¼ miles / 5.2km

Gradient: Flat

Severity: Easy

Approx. time to walk: 2 hours

Stiles: None

Map: OS Explorer 132 (Winchester)

Path description: Pavements, pedestrianised streets and paths

Start point: Chesil Street north car park (GR SU 487291)

Parking: Chesil Street north car park (SO23 0HU) (charges apply; free on Sundays)

Dog friendly: Yes, but keep on a lead where appropriate

Toilets: Abbey Gardens

Nearest food: River Cottage Canteen, Abbey Gardens

1. From the Chesil Street car park exit onto Chesil Street and walk along it to reach a T-junction with Bridge Street. Turn left, cross the bridge, then continue along the High Street.

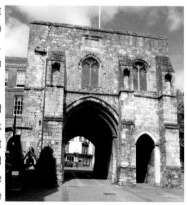

2. Keep ahead on the pedestrianised High Street passing Middle Brook Street on the right then Market Street on the left. Take the time to stop and enjoy the many old buildings and the Buttercross, which you will find on the left by The Pentice. Then keep ahead to the Lloyds Bank building with its rather spectacular protruding clock on the left. Then have a look at the God Begot House opposite it. Also check out the building on the left on the corner of High Street and St Thomas Street. It's now a branch of Joules but of you look closely you will see that it was once Ye Dolphin Inn. Then continue to cross Southgate Street, pass Trafalgar Street on the left and the offices of BBC Radio Solent, to reach the historic Westgate.

3. Just before you reach the gate bear left heading towards The Great Hall. Admission is free but donations are welcome. Walk round the Hall, look at the table then exit through a side door into the re-creation of Queen Eleanor's 13th-century garden. Turn right then climb up some steps, exit onto the street to turn left to follow the signs pointing to the cathedral.

4. Walk through the gardens of Peninsula Square surrounded by the magnificent military museums buildings, then cross to the left-hand corner to go down some steps. Turn left to pass through Beaumont Green then turn right, followed by left and right turns to pass by a church and reach a T-junction at the foot of Archery Lane.

5. Turn left, cross the road then turn right down some steps and along St Thomas' Passage heading in the direction of the cathedral tower. At the T-junction turn

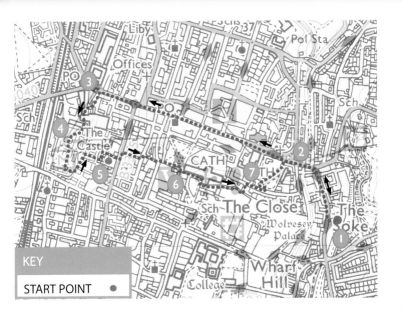

left opposite Mulberry House, pass Mason's Yard on your left then turn right into Minster Lane. When it ends cross over Little Minster Streete then head along Great Minster Street and on into the cathedral grounds.

6. Turn right in front of the cathedral then left to walk round the outside anti-clockwise. When the path reaches the end of the cathedral continue along it to reach a T-junction, and turn right along Colebrook Street.

7. A short distance along this street will bring you to River Cottage Canteen on the left. Turn left here just past it to enter Abbey Gardens, turn left in front of River Cottage, cross a footbridge and follow either of the paths to reach a gate onto High Street. Turn right here and re-trace your outward journey to return to the car park.

iStock

iStock

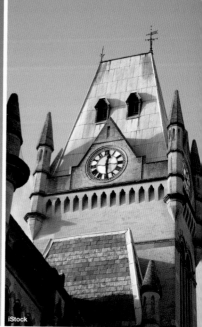

iStock

ABOUT THE AUTHORS

Moira McCrossan and Hugh Taylor are a husband and wife writing team now specialising in travel for the over 50's and walking guides. They are also travel editors of the UK's premier over 50's web site laterlife.com.

Moira McCrossan spent most of her working life in education and was a Primary School Head Teacher. An active trade unionist she is a former President of the Educational Institute of Scotland, served on the general council of the Scottish TUC and the executive committee of the Women's National Commission for whom she co-authored the report, Growing up Female in the UK. She was also a frequent contributor to the Times Educational Supplement (Scotland).

Hugh Taylor is an Award winning travel writer, broadcaster and photographer. He worked extensively for BBC Radio, producing several series for Radio 2 including Doomsday in the Afternoon about the music of the Scottish Travellers.

Together they have written or contributed to over forty travel and outdoor guides, some of which have been translated into several languages. They range from major country guides covering Scotland, Lebanon and Jordan to walking books throughout the UK. Their work has appeared worldwide in publications as diverse as The Times, Women's Realm, Choice, The Herald, Interval World and the Glencairn Gazette. They live in the picturesque southern Scottish village of Moniaive (www.moniaive.org.uk).

ACKNOWLEDGEMENTS

The authors would like to thank Rob Ganley, Andrew Robson and The Camping and Caravanning Club for providing us with a base from which to do the walks and the research for this book; the Managers and Assistant Managers at Horsley and Verwood Camping and Caravanning Club sites; and Steve and Judith Reed of Steve Reed Tourism (www.stevereedtourism.co.uk) for help and advice.